KENT
WINDMILLS
&
WATERMILLS

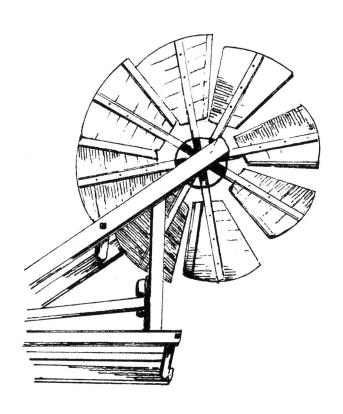

Gregory Holyoake.

KENT
WINDMILLS
&
WATERMILLS

Watercolours   TOM BURNHAM

Commentary   GREGORY HOLYOAKE

for
MIKE
& JENNY

Companion volume:
'DEAL & WALMER ~ A Celebration'

First published in an edition limited to 750 copies
in 2012 by The Dovecote Press Ltd
Stanbridge, Wimborne Minster, Dorset BH21 4JD

ISBN 978-1-904-34996-9

Designed by David Burnett
Photography by Liz Mott

Typeset in Sabon
Printed and bound by GraphyCems, Navarra

All the papers used by The Dovecote Press are natural, recyclable products
made from wood grown in sustainable, well-managed forests

A CIP catalogue record for this book is available
from the British Library

CONTENTS

Sandwich White Mill is a conspicuous smock mill that occupies its own meadow next to the railway crossing about one mile north-west of the medieval town. It dominates the landscape and looks particularly splendid when garlanded on highdays and holidays.

At the beginning of the 19th century there were six working mills within the town's boundaries although the White Mill is the sole survivor. Its companion, the Black Mill, was engulfed by flames in about 1910. Residents considered this to be God's judgment upon the miller who defiantly worked it every Sunday!

Probable date of its construction is 1760. Boys' *History of Sandwich* includes an engraving of a smock mill just outside the Canterbury gate in 1782. Hasted's map shows two mills – thought to represent the White and the Black – in the same area in 1799.

The White Mill was worked by wind until a steam engine was installed around 1900. Later, a diesel engine was substituted whose thudding motor could be heard in the middle of the town. Like similar general purpose mills, the White Mill ground wheat into flour for local bakers and housewives and produced food for farm animals from oats and barley. The mill finally closed in 1953.

Little is known of the early millers but it was acquired by a pair of brothers – Alfred and Thomas Stanley – in 1861. When Alfred moved to Temple Ewell, near Dover, Thomas remained at the White Mill. His five sons all became master millers in Kent but the youngest suffered a tragic death at Sandwich. Albert William was working inside the mill when his overcoat caught in a revolving shaft and he was dragged furiously round until fatally injured. The last miller was Albert Victor, Thomas Stanley's grandson.

The millers inhabited the cosy white washed cottage adjacent to the windmill. It was necessary to build long and low to avoid obstructing the free flow of the prevailing winds that would turn the sails. The compact building incorporated a bread oven behind the fireplace and a laundry equipped with stove, mangle, irons and stone sink.

Restoration of White Mill began under the expert guidance of Vincent Pargeter, supported by the Society for the Protection of Ancient Buildings and its new owners, Sandwich Town Council, in the 1960s. It is fitted with four double shuttered spring sweeps, two of which have unusual half-bow springs, and a gallery that allowed the miller to attend to his sails. Most machinery remains, including two pairs of stones, governors and a flour dresser. It is a sheer delight to watch the restored sails and fantail idle round in a moderate wind.

Today, White Mill is manned by a team of dedicated volunteers who frequently open it to visitors. They have accumulated a collection of rural and agricultural tools to recreate workshops – a cobbler's, a blacksmith's and a wheelwright's – and outbuildings, including a former wash house, cowshed, stables and a dairy, to present a fascinating folk museum.

Margate 'Draper's Mill' once formed the first – and last surviving – of a trio of mills in the vicinity.

This elegant smock mill stood alone until it was joined in about 1869 by a smaller smock removed from a site near the railway station at Barham. Each portion was carefully numbered as it was dismantled so that it could be easily re-erected on a new brick base. Inevitably, it became known as 'Little Draper's Mill'. When it was demolished in 1929, its base was retained and for a time became a garage.

A third mill on this site was known as 'The Pumper'. This large, powerful pumping mill was erected for the Corporation Waterworks around 1874. Originally, this tower mill had five sweeps but, when they were battered in a gale, their number was reduced to four.

Twenty years later, the pumping mill was tail-winded and severely damaged in a storm. The windshaft, midlings and sweeps were wrecked and proved too costly to repair. Sadly, after remaining capless for a number of years, this third mill was demolished.

The sole survivor, 'Old Mill', was built to grind corn in 1847 by John Holman of Canterbury. It is first depicted on the Ordnance Survey Map of 1853. It stands alongside a steeply sloping field where fragments of Roman pottery have been excavated.

This black tarred weather boarded smock mill with its familiar Kentish cap stands on a tall brick base. A notable feature is the long hanging string chain that controls the patent shutter sweeps. Adjacent is the former bakehouse which once enjoyed a flourishing trade by baking bread from the flour produced at the mill.

Much of the original machinery remain, including the three pairs of stones – two Derbyshire Peak and one French Burr – overdriven by the great spur wheel on the second floor.

The mill was driven by wind and steam until 1916 and then by an auxiliary gas engine until the mid 1930s. The sweeps were considered unsafe and had been removed, along with the fantail, in 1927. Gradually, the mill became obsolete and was abandoned.

'Old Mill' fell swiftly into decay and, further, was about to become swallowed up in a modern housing development. It stood in danger of demolition until conservationists were alerted by an astute headmaster, Mr. R.M. Towes. As chairman of Draper's Mill Trust, he was instrumental in raising funds for its restoration by millwrights, Phillip Lennard and Vincent Pargeter.

Happily, they restored the mill as a distinctive monument for Margate. The fantail was fitted in 1970 and the first pair of sweeps in 1971. Finally, the second pair was erected so that the sweeps now turn gaily in a gentle breeze.

Draper's 'Old Mill' houses a small exhibition of machinery from a former mill at Ash plus a modest display recording bygone windmills of Kent. Uniquely, it serves a significant educational role for schoolchildren in Thanet.

Sarre windmill is a fully working black tarred smock mill with a cap and fantail whose sails can be observed rotating gracefully across the flat open landscape of the Isle of Thanet. Situated on high ground slightly north-east of this hamlet famous for its cherry brandy, Sarre is known as 'the mill built eight miles from anywhere' because it is equidistant from Margate, Ramsgate, Sandwich and Canterbury.

It was built in 1820 by the Canterbury millwright, John Holman, who probably incorporated machinery from the redundant mill at nearby Monkton. It is a three storey smock standing on a two storey base although this was doubled in height to gain advantage of the coastal winds around 1856.

This complicated process involved raising the entire structure on jacks while the brickwork was built up underneath for one additional storey.

Sarre was the first windmill in Kent to be powered by an auxiliary steam engine, which occurred in 1861. This necessitated building an engine room, boiler house and brick chimney that stood as tall as the mill! It was replaced in 1907 by a gas engine installed in a subterranean passage.

Records reveal that Sarre Mill was active during the Great War when sacks of flour were delivered weekly to Chatham Barracks. Trading then ceased for a time and the sails were disconnected and fitted to the 'Union Mill' at Cranbrook. The millstones finally ground to a halt at the start of the Second World War when the structure was requisitioned as an observation post.

In 1985, Sarre Mill, which had fallen into advanced decay, was purchased by a neighbouring farmer, Malcolm Hobbs. As a youngster he had spent many happy hours cycling around the countryside, exploring the remaining mills of Kent. School holidays were passed blissfully in helping the miller at Chillenden postmill, near Nonnington. Advised by Vincent Pargeter, Malcolm began the mammoth task of restoring his newly acquired windmill to perfection.

Whole floors were renewed, fresh hoppers and shoes fitted, a gas engine installed and the pair of overdrift millstones – Derbyshire Peak and French Burr – professionally dressed. Original machinery was repaired including the great cast iron spur wheel, the composite brake wheel with its iron arms and wooden rim, and the cast iron wallower. Most importantly, a new cap and four sweeps were constructed – a challenging task for Mr Hobbs who was also a master carpenter. In 1991, this new pair of double patent sails turned for the first time to the delight of spectators.

Sarre Windmill remains one of Kent's very few remaining commercially viable windmills. The sprawling complex incorporates a farmyard museum and display of veteran lorries. Its new owners have introduced a mill shop selling high quality stone ground flour from locally grown wheat – when the wind blows!

Crabble Corn Mill at River near Dover is the last remaining working watermill in Kent. This imposing Georgian building with its massive iron wheel straddles the winding River Dour. Built in 1812, its purpose was to feed the troops garrisoned at Dover against the threat of invasion during the Napoleonic Wars.

The name indicates that a mill existed there from earliest times for crushing crab apples into cider. Henry III presented the Abbot of nearby St. Radigund's Abbey 'the site of the mill called Crabbehole'. In 1664, it was recorded that 'Crabbard Mill was by accident burnt down'. This was a timber watermill with a thatched roof so maybe the grindstones (running and bedding) collided causing a spark to ignite the highly combustible flour dust.

An insurance policy for a replacement
John Pilcher and Sons. The new mill
with a breastshot waterwheel, capable
It became one of about twenty mills
everything from beer to paper.

In the early 19th century, thousands of
to repel the threatened attack
contracted millers to
mills to supply the
New mills included
It is rumoured to
shipwrecked warships

This towering mill
Its breastshot wheel –
18 feet in diameter
with wooden floats
protected by a curved
five pairs of French burr
simultaneously, shaking the stout
timber floors.

mill dated 1788 lists the owners as
was a two storey timber building
of driving two pairs of millstones.
along this short river, supplying

troops were stationed around Dover
from France. Army victuallers
construct merchant flour
numerous military camps.
the present one at Crabble.
be constructed from
in Dover Harbour.
rose six storeys high.
seven feet across and
– was equipped
(or paddles) and
tin roof. It drove
stones which worked
brick walls and sloping

The mill enjoyed a thriving trade until the termination of the French Wars. Sadly, in 1842, its owner, John Webb Pilcher, was declared bankrupt.

Crabble Mill was then acquired by the ambitious Wilsher Mannering. He realised that London's expanding population would increase the demand for flour which could easily be shipped from Dover to the Capital. Trade expanded, Wilsher prospered.

At Crabble, Wilsher introduced the latest automated technology from America. Even so, the mill could not compete with the innovative steam power already installed at his second mill, Buckland. Inevitably, Crabble Mill closed in 1893.

A century later, Crabble Corn Mill Trust was formed to rescue this rare survival of the Industrial Revolution. A tour of the Victorian hydropowered automatic machinery reveals the process of refining the farmers' impure grain over six floors: the first grade was only suitable for animals; the second was served as gruel at the workhouse while the third refined flour – whitened with chalk – was offered to the local gentry.

Chillenden postmill stands – white and proud – with its skeletal sails among open wheat and barley fields near Wingham. This mill is unique because the stout wooden trestle framework supporting its timber body is completely exposed.

The mill was built by Holman's of Canterbury in 1868 and was the last of its type in Kent. It may, however, have re-used timber from an ancient postmill that occupied the same site but was blown down in a gale.

A windmill was marked on several early maps including Philip Symondson's (1596) and John Speed's (1611). Jane Austen would have noticed this earlier mill as she strolled along the country lanes when visiting close relatives at nearby Rowling or Goodnestone.

The postmill was owned by the wealthy and influential D'Aeth family. Legend asserts that one of the ladies ordered its construction on the present site after she had visited Holland. She wished to include a view of a windmill from the family's nearby stately home.

Subsequently, the D'Aeths and their successors leased the mill to tenant farmers. Early millers included William Hopper Bean (1887 – 1909) and Frederick Neves (1911 – 1920).

After that time, Albert Laker worked the mill for a quarter of a century. He lived at Miller's Farm in the village with his wife, Nell, and nephew, Norman. Norman started as an apprentice at the age of fourteen and rose to become Chillenden's last miller, retiring in the early 1950s.

This 'open trestle' postmill, although not perfectly balanced, was always well maintained. In 1927, for instance, one new midling and two new sails were fitted and the supporting beams of the trestle were repaired by the Holman Brothers. At one time, the whole structure canted forward and a trench had to be cut to facilitate the revolving sails.

Initially, it was fitted with two pairs of stones that ground either wheat for flour or grain for livestock until the end of the Second World War. It was then permanently disabled when strong winds carried off one of its canvas covered sweeps and it was thereafter incapable of operating by wind power. The postmill was later acquired and subsequently restored as a memorial to millwrights by Kent County Council.

Although it appears complete, the costly restoration necessitated the removal of part of the original equipment and the demolition of an adjoining barn. Chillenden mill is now actually fixed facing south-west. The brake wheel has been secured with iron straps to prevent the sails turning and the elliptical spring shutters lack their canvas coating.

Part of the machinery is striking feature is a cartwheel tailpole enabling the miller to turn his into the wind.

extant but the most attached to the sails more easily

Canterbury windmill is tucked discreetly away along a little lane atop St. Martin's Hill. Nonetheless, it occupies high ground and is therefore a landmark that can be viewed from several vantage points around the cathedral city.

At one time Canterbury was encircled by windmills. Splendid mills could be seen working at the surrounding villages of Bridge, Blean, Barham, Bekesbourne and Harbledown. The city, itself, boasted six windmills of which the one atop St. Martin's Hill is the sole survivor.

St. Martin's Mill consists of a white painted tapering brick tower – strong and elegant – with a large wooden Kent cap (an unique survivor on a tower mill in the county) but completely lacking sails. Built by John Adams in 1817, it was commonly known as 'Buck Windmill'.

A Tithe Map dated 1839 reveals that the mill and garden, which are drawn in detail, were then owned by Elizabeth Adams, presumably a relative. It was occupied by Thomas Marsh, who also milled at Cranbrook and Sissinghurst, while the surrounding Mill Field was farmed by John Collard.

A companion windmill stood on the south side of the Sandwich Road, almost opposite St. Martin's Mill, approximately where the 'Mill Inn' now stands. Known as the 'Black Mill', it was employed exclusively for milling cereal. It had a three storey smock on a two storey base with a stage at first floor level. There was one pair of shuttered sails and one pair of common sails. It was also winded by a fantail. In 1868, it was demolished and its machinery used for spare parts of nearby mills. St. Martin's Mill, however, continued to function until the beginning of the next century.

The rare Kent cap, many times repaired, has a curious raised louvred section. This feature was added when this tall stone structure served as an observation post during the Second World War. Later employment of the redundant mill was as a guest house with a honeymoon suite!

Today, the only pieces of machinery to survive are the cast iron windshaft and brake wheel. Once there were three pairs of stones but these were removed as novel garden ornaments. They were laid down in the pattern – the four and the three – cleverly imitating the constellation known as 'The Horse and Wagon'.

Around 1920, a Canterbury builder, Mr. Cozens, bought the mill and built the adjacent house in Windmill Close. It is built in high Gothic style with latticed windows, carved gables, steep roofs and a great storm porch. For a time this white painted, rendered building, became a restaurant known as 'Querns'. It is reputedly haunted.

Willesborough windmill, two miles east of Ashford, is one of the largest in south-east England. This white painted octagonal smock mill stands sentinel on a two storeyed square brick base with staging. It boasts four giant sweeps, a hoist, a cap and a fantail.

It replaced an earlier white painted smock mill that worked two cloth and two spring sails. There were four pairs of stones – three French burr and one Peak – plus a flour dressing machine. Apparently, its sails swung dangerously close to the ground.

The present mill was built for Messrs. Cornes by John Hill of Ashford and dates from 1869. Around 1920, after it became abandoned, it was acquired by William Manwaring. He employed an experienced miller, Mr Cobb, skilled at dressing the stones.

Often the sweeps were powerless to turn in the morning owing to a rich coating of ice after a 'silver frost'. Young Coltham, the apprentice, was then required to climb up each sweep from the timber stage at second floor level, using the open shutters as steps, while he chipped away at the ice with a pick.

Flour had not then been milled for many years. Previously, wheat, barley and maize were milled purely for livestock. Meal was delivered to the countryside in either an old Morris lorry or the horse drawn van, painted in typical millers' colours – yellow body, white canvas and red wheels. Often milling continued well into the night to make use of a good wind, although 'there was never milling on a Sunday', assured Mr Coltham upon his retirement.

Great care had always to be taken to use the door away from the revolving sweeps when walking from the mill interior onto the staging. Once, this led to a terrible accident when the miller's daughter stepped through the wrong door unaware of the approaching danger.

The mill was worked by wind power – its large four pairs of stones – until 1938. An electric power a fifth set of stones. Willesborough Mill World War.

patent sails driving those motor was then installed to worked until the Second

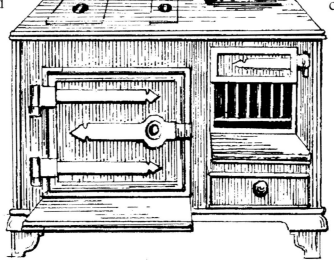

When the mill was sold to a building firm, had been penciled in idle moments upon the amusing scribble was dated 1882: 'Ground High wind. Miller

it was noted that a diary interior timbers. One found on the bin floor covered with snow. drunk'.

Throughout the owned by Tim builder who lived adjoining red brick this was used as a for the daughter Mill, Chatham.

1970s the mill was Robbins, an organ with his family in the cottage. At one time honeymoon cottage of the miller at Star

Ashford Borough this majestic produces its own

Council has restored structure and it now stone ground flour.

Westwell watermill is a charming feature of this ancient village, ablaze with daffodils each spring, four miles north-west of Ashford and nestling snugly under the Kent Downs.

Components of this perfect English village number a Victorian red brick schoolhouse on the corner of Gold Hill and an enticing pub opposite the green, 'The Wheel', whose novel sign is a waggon wheel. Its spokes are all white apart from one painted green as a reminder of two regular customers, members of the New Zealand Army, billeted nearby during the Second World War.

The 13th century Church of St. Mary, despite its coarse rendering and dumpy shingle spire, is considered to be one of the prettiest in Kent. Lift the latch (key in pub) and the visitor will be rewarded by a stunning interior. Treasures include heraldic glass from the reign of Richard II and a rare stained glass Tree of Jesse, that presents the descent of Christ from King David. A brass plaque recalls a former Vicar, Rev. Henry Honywood D'Ombrain, founder of 'The Rose Society' and 'The Horticultural Society'. He lived in the Vicarage, a high Victorian confection, approached via a carriage sweep through lawns strewn with wild violets and wood anemones.

Hidden away in a curve in the road and peeping from behind an undulating hedge is the picturesque watermill. This is a long, low, red brick building, partly weather boarded, with a red tiled hipped roof pierced at one end by a tall chimney stack. There is a profusion of latticed windows and a stable door directly below a sack hoist with a tiny balcony.

At one side is a sturdy overshot waterwheel, whose lichened paddles still thunder into action when fed from the millrace. A planked footbridge crosses the trickling stream to the duckpond while a Judas tree, with its blood-like, magenta-pink flowers, towers over the silky lawn.

Westwell 'Water Corn Mill', privately owned, is a Georgian building on a far older foundation. Originally, it was divided into two halves – the working mill and the miller's house. Today it makes a characterful residence. There is an abundance of step-through rooms with low beams, inglenook fireplaces and flagstone floors.

A sale catalogue for 1929 describes 'Lot 9': 'The Mill which is activated by a water wheel is divided into three floors. It has two mill stones and the top floor is filled with 9 bins. There is a sack hoist to all floors.' A description of a garden and orchard mentions pig pounds, two stall stables and loose box.

Fed from a chalk spring, the large mill pond at the rear is 'gin clear'. It provides a haven for wild birds: moorhens, mallards, woodpeckers, kingfishers, barn owls and, occasionally, a heron that sits and contemplates.

Woodchurch

Woodchurch windmill stands high and proud atop a gentle slope above the village five miles south west of Ashford and four miles east of Tenterden. From the summit there are views over the rich, rolling downland of the Weald of Kent and the distant coast of the English Channel.

Once there was a pair of identical smock mills, known affectionately as 'The Twins', standing in close proximity on this same hill, north of the village. The upper mill was called 'The Black Mill', thought to have been erected in about 1750, while the surviving lower or 'White Mill' dates from 1820. In 1860, both mills were purchased by the Tanton family from West Hougham, near Dover, in whose possession they thereafter remained.

The older mill dealt mainly with the rougher trade of grinding cattle and pig corn while the existing larger mill was reserved for the higher quality flour trade. Grinding corn continued until 1926 after which time both mills fell into disrepair.

The 'Black Mill' served as an observation post by the military throughout the First World War and as a tribute to this valiant wartime service a model aeroplane was affixed to its top. Apparently, the mill survived until the start of the Second World War.

'White Mill' has five floors, including the tall, ample black, tarred brick base surrounded by a robust new timber stage. Most of its machinery remains, including three sets of stones (two pairs of French burr and one pair of Peak.) Its hexagonal weather boarded smock has two pairs of sails and is surmounted by a Kent cap and fantail.

This prim, elegant mill has enjoyed a long and varied career. Originally, it sported cloth sails which were replaced by wooden patent ones acquired from two redundant neighbours – Aldington and High Halden – and it has employed several forms of auxiliary power, including a 7 h.p. portable steam engine. Just inside the store room at the base is parked a white coach owned by the last miller.

Woodchurch Mill is reached via a long, leafy lane through a kissing gate squeezed between two pubs – 'Bonny Cravat' and 'Six Bells' – opposite the 13th century All Saints' Church with its embattled weather walls and chubby tower, topped by a shingled broach spire. The mill stands idyllically among buttercup meadows, sheep pastures and wheatfields overlooking the village green with its white painted cricket pavilion.

Sir Sidney Nicholson, organist of Westminster Abbey, bequeathed 'White Mill' to the parish in 1947. Subsequently, it was acquired by Ashford Borough Council and almost completely restored by the gallant efforts of local craftsmen and enthusiasts, who now open it weekends in summer months.

Wittersham

'Stocks Mill' is named after the stocks that stood opposite, east of the village green, along the busy road from Rye to Tenterden. Today, the mill is concealed in a private garden with a trim lawn, surrounded by high hedges.

The mill is an impressive structure with its slender white wooden body containing three floors. It stands on a buttressed brick roundhouse with a long latticed window and a timber roof. There is a tailpost, lacking its wheel, protruding through the steep ladder at the rear, and four wide, spring shuttered sweeps that turn anticlockwise. The immense central oak post, on which the body of the mill revolves, is believed to be the strongest in England.

Its earliest history is a mystery. Carved inside the mill are the initials 'R.V.' and the date '1781' but these clues to its construction may be misleading. The mill is presumed to be far older and that it existed on an alternative site for decades. It was a common practice to transport this old type of post mill to a more favourable position where it would benefit from the prevailing winds. (Stocks Mill does not appear on maps until 1821.) Certainly, the mill was operational by 1792 when it was owned by Thomas Howars. A copy of his insurance policy shows that the premium paid was £250. A substantial sum reflecting a profitable business! Another early miller was Thomas Venus. Millers here tended to work a second postmill, that stood more centrally in a nearby meadow, in tandem. One miller who worked both mills was Richard Parton, left a widower with ten children, in 1838.

At the end of the 19th century, Miller John Holdstock posed for a photograph wearing torn trousers and rolled up sleeves yet sporting a bowler and a gold watch chain in his waistcoat pocket. By then Stocks Mill was uneconomical and it ceased to work.

Around 1900, it was purchased by the actor, Norman Forbes-Robertson, who came to reside in the splendid Mill House, previously a poorhouse. An early motorist, he employed his own chauffeur to whisk him away on country drives, often calling upon his neighbour, the actress, Ellen Terry, at Smallhythe.

During his residency, the roundhouse, sweeps and tailpost were restored and the body freshly painted. The ground floor was used as a garden shed; the first floor as a fruit store. The mill now formed a feature of a landscaped garden. Owls that took up occupancy in the upper storey seemed unperturbed by the rocking of the mill in high winds.

During the 1930s, the mill was used as a studio by the artist, Rudolph Helmut Sauter. He initiated further repairs after the structure was revealed to be in a parlous state.

Admiral Sir Edward Parry was in residence in the 1950s when the mill was equipped with four new sweeps, turned through 90 degrees annually to relieve the strain on them that immobility brought.

More recently, the mill has been cared for by successive residents of the Mill House. In 1974, Kent County Council authorised extensive restoration. Today, Friends of Stocks Mill welcome summer visitors to the tallest remaining postmill in Kent.

Sandhurst windmill is a spectacular new build of a rare five sailed octagonal smock mill. It stands proudly on a hummock, east of the village, on the border of Romney Marsh. This tall, slim, modern mill lacks internal machinery because it was purpose built as a novel home at the beginning of the 21st century.

The original smock mill was the only five sweep corn mill known to have been built in Kent.

It was constructed in 1844 for James Collins on his farm known as 'Ringle Crouch Green' by the celebrated millwright, George Warren, of Hawkshurst. Unsurprisingly, it was hailed as 'Warren's Masterpiece'. Upon its completion, one of his young sons, an apprentice, triumphantly stood on his head on top of the cap!

Apparently, the construction of a five sailed mill was a challenge to Warren who travelled to the north of the country to seek a pattern. A local story relates how James Collins wanted to prove that he was better than his neighbours by building a mill with five sails and, he vowed, should a rival built one with six he would built one with seven! In fact, a six sweep mill was erected at Great Chart near Ashford, but by that time Collins had died.

Certainly, Sandhurst windmill was a splendid example of the millwrights' craft. It had six storeys with a stage, single shuttered sweeps and a fantail. There were four pairs of stones which might all be turned simultaneously with a strong wind: two for wheat, one for cracking corn and another for grinding oats. The brick base was painted red and the body of the mill white.

Collins enjoyed a roaring trade working Sandhurst in conjunction with a watermill across the border at Bodiam. His two young sons also became millers: Edward, inherited this windmill while Tom worked Benenden Mill. Their seven elder sisters sought employment elsewhere.

Edward Collins worked the mill until he died about 1911. His two sons, Edward and Harry, declined to carry on the family business and hired out the mill to C.J. Bannister. He abandoned Sandhurst and transferred the stones to his main mill at Northiam.

Milling ended, the structure became derelict. One of the sweeps was blown away in a high wind and used for preventing cattle from straying into a pond; the fantail and shutters were removed and the staging was dismantled. Village lads regarded it as a playground.

The body of the mill was removed after the Second World War. This paved the way for the present mill on the same site but which bears little resemblance to the original one. It has a mellow pink brick base, white octagonal smock, wide wooden staging, profusion of sash windows, no fantail but a cap a size too large and those gleaming five (fixed) sails.

Chilham's watermill, which straddles the River Stour, is a grand Victorian affair that lies hidden a short distance south of the picturesque village. It is the last surviving of six mills located in this vicinity recorded in Domesday Book.

The present magnificent flour watermill, rebuilt in the mid 19th century, is a five storeyed affair, built of red brick with white weather boarding. Owned by the Mid Kent Water Board, it has been beautifully restored and now presents a perfect example of early industrial architecture. It is considered to be the best conserved watermill in Southern England.

The complicated machinery, built almost entirely of timber, remains in perfect working order and can still be turned by a single iron shaft – a testament to the skill and ingenuity of local engineers. Chilham was equipped with an 'undershot' waterwheel, common for river watermills without a great head of water.

Locally, the original structure was referred to as the 'French Mill' because five of its six pairs of stones were the composite type known as French burr, perfect for grinding fine flour. Handcarts regularly transported its flour to the quaintly named village, Old Wives Leas, where the ladies insisted that it was essential for them to bake their best bread.

The watermill has been owned throughout the centuries by the Lords of the Manor of Chilham, although at times ownership has been claimed by successive monarchs, including Henry VIII.

At one time a steam engine supplemented the water wheel as a source of power. This necessitated the installation of a massive chimney for the boiler, which rose several feet higher than the mill.

Flour was produced until 1934 when the mill was sold together with the miller's cottages, stables and wagon shed as a residence and the millstream was cultivated to grow watercress. The days when wheat was grown, milled and baked into bread in the

same village, alas, were gone
known for their longevity.
Chilham for an incredible
welcome retirement in 1925.
had been the village
Mid Kent Water
area was a good source
duly installed their pumping
watermill can be inspected
the extensive woodland
rewarding nature trail.
Kingfishers, finches and
banks; carp and tench
extensive lakes nearby are
provide licensed fishing.
downs above the densely
a neolithic long barrow (a
known as Julieberrie's Grave.

forever. Millers, by tradition, are
Joe Jordan worked as miller at
sixty-nine years before his
His daughter, Christiana,
schoolmistress for forty years.
Authority discovered that the
of high quality water and
equipment. Their rural
upon prior application while
surrounding the site offers a

bluetits all inhabit the river
swim in the millstream and
stocked with trout which
Concealed in the chalk
wooden Stour Valley is
great rarity) popularly

Cranbrook

'Union mill' – at seventy feet high – is the tallest smock mill in England. It rises over rooftops in this Wealden market town famous for its cloth industry. Its majestic stature has long been acknowledged. It was the first windmill to be listed (1949).

Apparently, the mill, constructed by James Humphrey, was required to be this tall to avoid the wind turbulence caused by the surrounding shops and houses on the adjacent hilltop. Further fine mills across the Kent countryside, all constructed by the same millwright, have vanished. (A sideline of his was hanging church bells.) Upon completion, Humphey's son balanced precariously on top of the mill cap and blew a bugle to announce free beer for a grand celebration!

Today, Cranbrook's Mill stands sentinel at the end of a wide lane – 'Russell's Yard' – bordered by ancient cottages whose gardens are planted with country flowers. The mill cannot fail to impress. A black tarred brick base encloses three storeys before even the staging is reached. The octagonal white, tapering, timber smock frame encompasses a further four storeys. There are four white sweeps, a Kent cap and a fantail. At night this magnificent structure is floodlit.

The mill was built in 1814 for Mary Dobell at around £1,500. She installed her son, Henry, as miller. Alas, there was a time of economic depression after the Napoleonic Wars which resulted in Mary's bankruptcy. The mill was acquired by five of her creditors who formed their own union to work the mill. Hence the name: 'Union Mill'.

Two brothers – John and George Russell – bought the mill in 1832. Immediately, they made tremendous improvements. Shuttered sweeps replaced the original common canvas ones, wooden cog wheels and gearing with ironwork, the manual chain to turn the cap with a fantail. (The large winding wheel is still present at the side of the cap.)

For fifty years the three pairs of stones (two remain) were powered solely by wind. About 1863 a steam engine was installed allowing extra stones to be turned. In 1919, this was superseded by a suction gas plant and in 1954 by an independent electric motor. The milling of flour, rice and barley was replaced by grain for livestock, although the mill has always remained in full mechanical order.

The last of the Russell family, another John, acquired 'Union Mill' in 1918. He further restored the mill, single handedly, to resume its viable milling business. Oddly, he retained windpower although he admitted that the wind never earned him any profit.

Wartime shortages caused John Russell to sell the mill for a pittance to Kent County Council. 'Union Mill' was restored to its former glory and is now cared for by Cranbrook Windmill Association. Today, visitors to the historic mill may purchase flour milled by windpower exactly as it did in Victorian times.

Meopham's 'Killick's Mill' is a distinctive feature of this charming village situated high on the North Downs. It stands in a garden next to the triangular green where cricket has been played since the late 18th century.

The mill was built in 1801 by the three Killick brothers who hailed from Strood. Reputedly, oak timbers came from from a dismantled battleship at Chatham Dockyard. The Killicks were millers and millwrights and they built their elegant mill to secure commissions.

Meopham is one of the smallest surviving mills in Kent. Consequently, it contains machinery of less than average dimensions. The wooden brake wheel is only 6 feet 6 inches in diameter. This is necessary to fit into the cramped cap, just twelve feet across!

Throughout its long life the mill was worked by only two families. The Killicks ran their mill, grinding corn by wind, until 1889. They then sold it to John Norton who worked the mill with his nephew, William. John's son, Leslie, helped while his two younger brothers delivered flour by donkey cart around farms until the outbreak of the Great War.

Immediately, it was commandeered for milling flour for troops but later food for livestock. When his father died, Leslie continued to operate the business alone until the mill finally went out of commission shortly after World War Two.

The mill worked solely by wind power until 1927. Afterwards, it was operated by an auxiliary engine and electric motor which resulted in the sweeps and fantail remaining motionless. At this period the mill created its own electric light.

Meopham Mill is a tapering three storey smock on a two storey sound brick base. It is hexagonal in plan, a feature which was shared by only two other Kent mills (Strood and Lower Stoke). There is a stage at second floor level. It has four double patent sails carried on a cast iron windshaft and it is winded by a fantail.

Originally, there were just two pairs of underdrift millstones. Later, a third and fourth pair of stones were added. A rare feature is the bell alarm that warned when the hopper was short of grain. This prevented them from 'running dry' and thus avoided the risk of fire from sparks caused by the friction of the touching surfaces.

In 1950, Meopham Mill was transferred to Kent County Council. Sussex millwrights, Messrs. E. Hole and Son, were commissioned to renovate it. The machinery, non operational, remains intact. It is now administered by a Trust. Inside, there are displays of milling tools and mill tokens. A unique feature is that the base serves as the office of Meopham Parish Council.

Rolvenden

Rolvenden is a rare example of an 18th century postmill. (A date 1772 is carved on the timber frame.) It seems certain, however, that a postmill mill has occupied this site since the mid 16th century.

This privately owned veteran corn mill stands prominently in lush farmland on an ancient mound just outside the straggling, village alongside the Rolvenden to Benenden Road.

It is a symmetrical, black, tarred, weather boarded postmill with four white common sails that once swiveled confidently on a single storey brick roundhouse, roofed in timber. (This is commonly known as a 'turret type'.) The body was turned into the wind via a tail pole or tiller beam, now rigidly anchored. Both the access ladder and wheel are missing.

Tithe Maps reveal the names of early millers: Thomas Record (1834); Richard Reeves (1839) and Thomas Gybbon Monypenny, a member of a prominent landowning family. Later this postmill was owned by John Greenhill, 'miller and grazier', who worked it profitably but then it was acquired by Horace Dunk who abandoned the business in 1883. Afterwards, it was acquired by Miller Collins although his purpose was to close Rolvenden in order to drum up more trade for his own impressive five sweep mill at Sandhurst.

Perhaps a little grinding was still carried out since Rolvenden Mill is thought to have continued operating until 1885. After this time the mill went rapidly into decline and a pair of sails were removed. During the First World War, the roundhouse was dismantled for firewood. This left the massive timber trestles that carried the centre post exposed to the elements. The mill lay forlorn and idle.

Between the wars, this quaint, gaunt postmill fell into dereliction: the crowntree had became misshapen and the windshaft dropped alarmingly; the framing of the breast was decayed while the flooring of the first floor collapsed.

In 1956 Rolvenden Mill was lovingly renovated by its new owners, Mr. and Mrs. Barham, in memory of their teenage son, John Nicholas, who was tragically killed in a road accident. The extensive repairs, which included renewal of interior framework, weatherboarding and sweeps, plus rebuilding the brick roundhouse with a timber roof, was undertaken by the Lincolnshire millwrights, Messrs. Thompson and Son.

Rolvenden Mill now looms tall and proud beside the converted granary, mill pond, cattle meadows and rolling hills that are slowly shrouded by evening mist while long shadows brush the silken grass in the late autumn sunshine. The interior, which is not open to the public, retains much of its original machinery, including two pairs of stones, one in the mill breast and the other in the tail, on the second floor.

Rolvenden Mill appeared in the musical film, 'Half A Sixpence', and it features on the wrought iron village sign.

Chart Gunpowder Mill formed part of a series of explosives factories at Faversham. First manufacture of 'black powder' (or gunpowder) began there around 1550, rendering it one of the oldest mills of its kind in the world. Chart mills were worked in turn by water, horses, steam and electricity.

Chart Mill in its present form, however, dates from around 1740 when it was incorporated into the Royal Powder Mills. Probably, gunpowder from there was used by troops at Trafalgar and Waterloo in the French Wars. Later, the industry expanded with the production of high explosive guncotton during the Great War. Gunpowder was not reserved for warfare since it had enabled routes to be blasted for canals and railways in the Industrial Revolution.

Gunpowder was manufactured there in the traditional manner invented by the Chinese. Key ingredients – saltpetre, sulphur and charcoal – already handmixed to the correct proportions, were crushed for about four hours by heavy rollers. They were then broken into grains of different sizes, dusted and glazed with graphite to render them impervious to moisture.

At Faversham, watermills were placed in sequence along streams – the tailrace of one feeding the headwater or millpond of the next – rising from the North Downs. Navigable tidal creeks (Faversham and Oare) allowed ingredients to be imported by sea from the Continent. Also, the finished product could be loaded onto ships for dispatch to Chatham Dockyard, Woolwich Arsenal and the Tower of London.

Chart Mills formed part of the Home Works (the first in the town) but there were also Oare and Marsh Works. This factory covered a vast area – now swallowed up in housing – that ironically became a place of beauty. Dense woodland served a dual purpose: alder and willow were planted for charcoal while forming a natural blast wall. Water courses provided power and were essential for fire fighting.

Explosions were frequent. Townsfolk constantly complained when minor blasts lifted their roofs and shattered their windows. A tiny spark was enough to cause a major incident and one horrendous accident killed 120 people.

Safety was paramount. Horses for transport were shod with copper shoes and railway tracks were formed of wood in danger zones. Tools were made of non ferrous metals. Even the protective clothing of the workmen lacked pockets in case they held matches.

Faversham Mills were closed in 1934 when manufacture of guncotton, cordite, TNT and dynamite was discontinued in favour of more modern factories. The mills were relocated to Scotland although manufacture of gunpowder has now ceased in Britain.

Chart Mill, despite an order for demolition, was spared and restored by The Faversham Society. This unique mill, with its exposed low breastshot iron waterwheel and original covered machinery, remains operational, given a suitable water supply. It is the only surviving gunpowder mill in Britain.

TOM BURNHAM is an admired artist whose charming watercolours are avidly collected. Brought up in Bath, Tom trained in graphic design at the renowned Bath Academy of Art. Later, his responsibilities as a manager for British Rail brought him into Kent where he was required to supervise the transport of materials for the construction of the Channel Tunnel. At that time, he and his family visited Deal and they fell in love with the place so much that they decided to settle there. Apart from recording the locality in the medium of watercolour, Tom is greatly involved in the local community. He is a stalwart member of Walmer Lawn Tennis Club and the Shotokan Karate Club. (He is a black belt!) He is also Secretary of the Deal and Walmer Inshore Fishermen's Association. Tom's wife, Marlene, was a former Town Mayor while their twin sons, Ben and Jack, are among the few remaining commercial fishermen on Deal Beach. Tom has been faithfully restoring a veteran pleasure boat, *Lady Irene*, now beached on the seafront adjacent to Deal Castle. This historic craft is probably one of the oldest, and certainly the most complete, beach boats in Britain. Tom's first art book was *Deal and Walmer ~ a Celebration*.

GREGORY HOLYOAKE is an actor, author and a schoolteacher who also lives in Deal. He trained as a schoolmaster at Culham College of Education, Oxfordshire, where he gained teaching diplomas in English Literature and Divinity. As an actor he trained at Rose Bruford College of Speech and Drama, Kent, before embarking on a theatrical career, appearing in repertory and repertoire countrywide. Gregory has been a photo journalist for forty years and he has appeared regularly in such prestigious national magazines as *Country Life*, *Country Homes and Interiors*, *This England*, *The Lady*, *Illustrated London News*, *Heritage* and *Evening Standard*. For five years he was chief reporter for *Kent Life* when he became an authority on Kentish Subjects. He photographed *Kent - The County in Colour* for Dovecote Press and *Scarecrows* for Unicorn Press. He has also written a trilogy of local histories – *Deal: Sad Smuggling Town*, *All In The Downs* and *Wellington At Walmer*, while his boyhood in postwar Kent is described in detail in *The Prefab Kid*. Gregory and Tom's first collaboration was *Deal and Walmer ~ a Celebration*.